bluebird

bluebird

Poems

James Crews

GREEN WRITERS PRESS | *Brattleboro, Vermont*

Printed in the United States

10 9 8 7 6 5 4 3 2 1

Green Writers Press is a Vermont-based publisher whose mission
is to spread a message of hope and renewal through the words and
images we publish. Throughout we will adhere to our commitment to
preserving and protecting the natural resources of the earth. To that
end, a percentage of our proceeds will be donated to environmental
activist groups. Green Writers Press gratefully acknowledges support
from individual donors, friends, and readers to help support the
environment and our publishing initiative.

Giving Voice to Writers & Artists Who Will Make the World a Better Place

Green Writers Press | Brattleboro, Vermont
www.greenwriterspress.com

ISBN: 978-1-9505845-5-0

Illustration by Anne Hunter.
annehunterstudio.com

COVER ART:
"Cider Mill Road" by Stella Ehrich.
stellaehrich.com

The paper used in this publication is produced by mills committed
to responsible and sustainable forestry practices.

for Brad, once again and always

CONTENTS

PART ONE

*We are like someone in a very dark night over whom
lightning flashes again and again.*

—MAIMONIDES

Fireflies

Some insights come like lightning—
blinding and fierce—while others arrive
as firefly-flashes that brighten only
an inch or so of air around them.
Yet even these can gather power
over time, like the summer night
I woke and stood at the window
to watch all that pulsing outside—
like thousands of prayers flaring up
above the houses, saying *here*
and *here* and *here*, as I made my way
down the stairs using only the light
of those small bodies to guide me.

The Blessing

The shadow figure leaned over the bed
where I lay, halfway between sleep
and dream, and kissed me on the cheek.

I should have felt frightened, and recoiled
at the sight of that not-quite-man with fire
for eyes, but I recognized the tender glance

and knew it was my father who'd come back
to give his blessing for this life I've chosen—
of visible stars and the ticking woodstove

and moonlight on snow like a skin-tight
blue dress the fallow fields slip on at night
when no one's looking. And for the man

sleeping next to me, his breath building
a rhythm that could calm any ghost or beast.
I woke with that kiss still on my cheek,

alive and burning so I'd remember.

Living Light

Any new life you claim
is like a handmade table
with nothing on it
but an empty cup and bowl
and the sun streaming in
like the gaze of a god
glad you took this leap of faith.

A place was set for you
long ago at this table
built of an old barn door
still bearing the pockmarks
of nail-holes, the scars
of years spent exposed to snow.

All you have to do
is pull out a chair, choose
to stay in this place
where hope fills the air like pollen.
Just sit here with coffee
and let the living light of day
wrap its warmth around you—
a thin but invincible skin.

Tablet

I thought nothing of ripping out a page
from the little blue spiral-bound notebook
my husband keeps on the coffee table—
until I saw the imprints of previous words
he'd written in his usual capital letters:
the note he slipped into my overnight bag,
tucking it into my jeans pocket so I'd find it
when I put them on the next morning,
or the message he left on the counter because
I wasn't feeling well, telling me he'd driven
all the way to town to buy the spicy lentil soup
now waiting for me in the fridge. His ghost letters
looped together and blended with each other,
but I could still make out the obvious words
like *SOON* and *BABE*, his exclamation points.
I'd meant to use the paper for a grocery list
but couldn't force myself to mar the surface
of what now seemed an artifact: I held it up
to the sunlight and traced the places where
the pen-tip had carved his name at the bottom
like an ancient stylus pressing into wet clay
the oldest love poem ever found.

Scrap of Paper

Every day is a journey, and the journey itself is home.
                                              —Matsuo Bashō

Bashō tells me that once it is finished
I should see this poem as nothing more
than a scrap of paper stained with
the finch-prints of a few lines of black ink.

But I ripped this page from a notepad
with my own hand, laid it on the table
made by my father-in-law out of barn boards
from a farm in Salem, New York.

This morning, I swore I could still smell
hay being forked into a sun-warmed loft,
and thought I could hear every dizzying blow
of a hammer driving nails into this weathered wood.

It shouldn't matter, but each of these words
has a history, and though this piece of paper
will be placed in the recycling bin,
soon to be crushed into pulp, and later turned

into paper again, I take comfort in knowing
that, for a while at least, it will carry
traces of my DNA in the spots of coffee
spilled at the edges where I stopped to wonder

what comes next.

Rikpa

There is a mind behind the mind—
smaller perhaps, and much simpler.
Rikpa, the Tibetans call it, meaning
brightness or *intelligence*—meaning
we are not always what we think.
Inside this mind, no chattering voice
reminds me to buy dish soap and bread.
No nightly worries streak across the screen
of my dreaming eyes like lightning
splitting the sky. Here, the black-banded
wings of fear flap at my back only
when my life is actually in danger.
Sometimes, I feel my *rikpa* trying
to shine through—a streetlamp too weak
to burn off the nimbus of fog around it.
Sometimes, when I remember to pause
on my walk down these dirt roads,
I notice the dew-soaked spider webs
as wide as dinner plates among
the waving reeds, and when I sit alone
on the screened-in porch without
a book, notebook, or phone
the mountains can speak to me
with the silence stone knows best.

First Date, Hawk Mountain

We sat together on the grassy mountain
where the sun shone clear and hard
on our faces as we inched closer—
the stone beneath us soaking up our heat
and giving us back an ancient cold
that told of a love larger than the self.
I shivered when you took off my gloves
and kissed the hands that touched you
for the first time on top of that mountain
I knew we'd always carry within us—
muscle and bone of the place where birders
gather to trace the hawks' migration
as they cross overhead. I had this vision
of a thermal sweeping in and lifting us
into the same welcoming blue as soon as
our lips finally met. But when I came to,
we were still earthbound, of course,
seated on grass and leaves, eye to eye,
arm in arm, keeping each other warm.

Heat

Words can't capture the sensation
of actually kissing you, the fit
of lips made for each other.
Language fails me as it never has,
lifting from my mind like heat
rising from the baseboard and leaving
metal that stays hot to the touch
only so long before going cold.
But surely in the middle of the night,
like me, that heater remembers
what it's like to feel something
so pulsing, electric, and real
shooting through every wire inside
and warming the whole room.

Sauna

After an hour of sweating, pouring water
on stones in the stove over and over
and breathing the heat that surrounded me,
I stepped out in the night and leaped
with a splash into the icy pond below.
But I had to stay in the shock of that freezing
water for longer than I wanted before
my legs would flail again, before my eyes
sprang open, and I forced my arms
upward, reaching with my whole being
for the worn wood of the dock with which
to lift my body out of the blackness—
more alive now and beaming, my skin
steaming like warm pavement the moment
a snowstorm begins to transform it.

The Price

Snow gathers on the antler-branches.
A few brave cars carve twin tracks
on blacktop still hoarding its heat.
I want to go back to sleep, stop
thinking about my mother rolled out
of surgery, wondering how much pain
she's in, if she's calling my name.
And whether or not my husband's plane
will be late tonight, will stay in the sky
and skid safely to a halt on a runway
free of black ice. It is the price of love—
this worry that fills the ravaged yard,
piling quite silently against my life
no matter how warm I keep the house,
how much salt I spread around it.

Annunciation on Rue Saint-Urbain

The silence was so complete that night
on the street in Montréal, I could hear
snow snapping beneath our feet
like bubble wrap popping with each
new step. Now, his voice told me,
everything's been changed, rearranged.
Like that moment the angel Gabriel
flew down to whisper in Mary's ear:
*There's something bright in you that wasn't
there before.* Inside, frost-flowers bloomed
on the windows—the glass that cold—
and our bodies kept interlocking
in the snow-light that filled the room.

Winter Offering

We must learn to give without reason,
offer all that we have, even if
the gift seems too meager.
Like these heels of stale bread I slip
in my coat pocket and take outside
for the crows perched in the bare maple
by the driveway—six starved soldiers
standing guard in a ruined cathedral.

I break the bread into smaller pieces,
place them on an overturned crate
in the field, then call the crows—
not knowing if they will understand,
not knowing if they will come closer
and accept the hunks of old sourdough
already beginning to soften
in the softly falling snow.

The Present

The gift doesn't always arrive
tied with ribbon,
wrapped in tissue paper.
It can be as plain
as the glass of orange juice
your father poured for you
just before he died
and left on the kitchen table—
how you drank from it for years.

Or the rustling of cattails
in the marsh beside the road
as a muskrat slips through
that clear water
and drops you like an anchor
into the center of yourself.

It is the wool blanket
draped across your lap—
every pill of white fuzz
you pick from it when worried—
and the urge to reach out
and rub the arm of a friend
about to start radiation again.

It is the present
of enough time and space
to look into her tired face
and see the eyes of a child
staring back at you
through the fear.

Night Dweller

When the thumb of fear lifts, we are so alive.
                    —Mary Oliver

Fear tries to keep you small,
presses you under its wide thumb

so you never want to leave the house,
make the phone call, ask for help.

But sometimes you pry yourself loose,
slip out into the winter night

and pass through a shimmering black tunnel—
no moon, no stars, no flashlight—

where anything might happen, and does;
where your body might fail you, and does.

You fall to your knees and listen
to the scuffing noise of leftover leaves

on the beech trees, calling with each rustle:
Be more like us. Dwell naked

in the night without running away.
Hear what secret languages you learn

by staying. See what sweeping thoughts
perch in each of your branches.

Leave No Trace

We break branches and make tracks
on trails that keep the shape
of our boot-soles as we rub stones
that look like faces lifted
out of loam by the talon-like
root-claws of maples growing up
over them—and then we touch the trees.
Leave no trace, we've been told,
though we know this is impossible
when we abandon countless breaths,
threads of conversation
and stray hairs snagged on thorns
which some warbler will soon
swoop in and steal, weaving
pieces of us into her tufted nest
tucked deep inside a willow
we'll never see.

At Stratton Pond

If you've ever sat on the dock
near a pond and watched for hours
as salamanders flit in the shallows,
as algae fronds dance back and forth
in time with the current, unfurling
every part of themselves for the water—

then you know what it means to move
in real time, to feel yourself inside the caves
the arched algae makes for tadpoles
and minnows to swim through. You know
how noon sun warms the tops of beech trees
so each branch gives up its sleeve
of ice, like glass falling from a chandelier.

You've seen it melt into copper leaf-litter,
water sinking through softened soil
to touch the roots of trout lilies
about to bloom—and now blooming when you
pass through again on your way back to the car.

You've learned to take your time, stopping
to rub those tender places on birches
where the ancient scrollwork of bark
has peeled back to reveal the secret
of all existence: To live unbound by time
and mind—to grow, speak, touch and taste
at a pace that feels more real.

Altars of Attention

Someone has stacked rock cairns
on top of stumps and stone walls
all along the washed-out road
I walk this morning. Each slab
is balanced by the other like one
right action holding space for the next.
But what is the message of these
small towers shored against the
mossy ruins of a country road?
Are they evidence of an effort
solid enough to withstand wind,
lashing rain and the shrapnel
of beer cans tossed from trucks?
I want to kneel and touch each one,
feel how the tip of one stone
fits into the divot of another,
but I don't. Let them be altars
of attention that testify: someone
paused here and cared enough
to build these for no reason other
than the pleasure of making them.

Clearly

To see clearly,
not needing a drink
or pill or puff
of any pipe
to know I'm alive.
To come home,
peel off sandals
and step onto
the cool tile floor
needing only
the rush of water
over strawberries
I picked myself
and then a knife
to trim the dusty
green heads
from each one,
to watch them
gleam cleanly
in a colander
in a patch of sun
next to the sink.

Ye Tang Che

When you're more tired
than you've ever been,
and you're fed up with
consuming all the news—
endless voices streaming
from each of your screens—
when you've had it with
nightly glasses of wine
to dull the day's noise
and pills to grease the track
that leads to white sleep,
when you're at the end
of your rope, just hanging
over the steep edge
of the cliff of your life,
chased on all sides
by the tigers who stalk
above and below—
then you are at last
ye tang che, as the Tibetans
say, meaning exhausted
and freed from the hope
that there's something
more to be. You can
reach out, pick the strawberry
growing in front of you
and place it in your mouth,
enjoying every bite
without sugar or cream,
even while the tigers
keep nipping at your heels.

Adoration

Don't call this world adorable, or useful, that's not it.
                                        —Mary Oliver

Since our first days swaddled in sheets,
we've been leashed to the chaos
of freeways, skyscrapers, and jetliners,
to the cracked concrete out of which the crown
of a single dandelion shoots up. Wait long enough,
that weed will go to seed, will blow off
and ride a gust of wind to the farthest reaches,
finding a new home in loose soil.
But for now, it's rooted beneath the stamping,
stumbling feet of thousands of passersby,
and like us, risks being crushed simply by existing.
We pass through this crowded city called life
with seat belts, yes, with helmets,
deadbolts, bulletproof vests, car alarms—
but with precious little protection.
Don't call this world adorable unless
you mean we were summoned here to love
and relish and worship in brief stretches
of ecstasy—for the falling leaf,
for dust tumbling a galaxy through sunshine.
For the sharp and glinting edges of a spoon
scooping maple yogurt out of the container.
For a lover's curls bunched at the back of his neck,
blond hair shimmering in the lengthening
and harsh summer light.

Here on Earth

This morning, I came upon
a strand of his blond hair
standing straight up on his pillow
in a patch of sun from the skylight.

The sight of it stopped me—
it could have been a piece
of woven gold placed in the slight
imprint where his head had rested last night.

Of course, it wasn't, and looking closer,
I found several more hairs there,
just as golden, then went so far as to
get down on my knees to examine them.

I tell you, I was changed by the presence
of a few of my husband's lost hairs
waving in the wind of my breath.
I kept thinking about how close I'd come

to never seeing them, how if I turned
my head an inch to the right or left
I saw nothing but the blank field
of a slept-on, sun-struck pillow.

And what would I be, and who
would we be without moments like these
to remind us just how thin our time is
here on earth.

PART TWO

We are poor students who stay after school to study joy.

—ROBERT BLY

Ripples

When the sun came up over the mountains
at precisely 6:19 A.M., I saw
inside the window pane the concentric circles
of a web it took all night to spin.
First, amazement—then the poison
of comparison: What do I build
that is so intricate, that requires so much
undivided attention? Not these words
scrawled in a spiral-bound notebook,
not the quiche I made last night for supper
or the tomatoes I grow. All things
which fade or end or must be consumed.
I came back to the table hours later
and found the web gone, folded up like a tent.

It is not lost on me that this life
I'm now making, far from any place I've known
might be the intricate thing I'm seeking,
the interlocking rings of which
will touch others, joy always threading
itself to joy. Today, I'll walk
these undriven gravel roads until I can
go no further. I'll stop to feast
on tiny black raspberries and listen
to frogs leaping back into the shaded puddle
that never evaporates. Slowness
will seep into my hurried bones,
and I'll rest on the banks of the pond,
my mind at last like the head
of the snapping turtle breaking the surface
for air, and sending wave after wave
back to shore where my only question now
will be whether or not to leap in
and add my ripples to his.

Enough

I plead with the god of good enough today:
let me hear rain and not think of the hikes
I will miss, the muddy lane it will make of our driveway.
Let me listen instead and say: *Enough.*

Let me imagine the cold needles of water
slipping beneath the carpet of newly green grass
to touch the roots of wildflowers and trees
at last awakened by days of steady sun.

Let me think, *enough*—not like a mantra
but a prayer that comes more naturally,
springing from the folds of my mind
like the simplest memory. We were shaped

for praise, our bodies built of the flesh and bones
of thanks for this unknowable force
that animates us, that wants us to cut a path
through the world's clutter and distraction

to that bright place of everlasting light inside.
Enough this stained lampshade, the glow
that fills the room. Enough these ashes leaking
from the woodstove I haven't cleaned in weeks.

Enough the floorboards and pine beams
that hold up the house, splitting and popping
in the night like some god knocking, saying,
Please, let me into your life.

Biblia Sacra

I think of those illiterate scribes
copying the Latin of the Bible
onto sheets of vellum the color
of autumn sun or clover honey
or bread just pulled from the oven.
They could not understand
what they wrote, but trusted
that others would cherish the pages,
would pray over their ink-marks
in the small hours of the morning,
a finger tracing the holy words
pressed into skin they blessed
over and over with the tip of a pen.

Practice

Whether meditation or prayer,
I call what I do each day *practice*
because I know I'll always be a novice

seated at the piano, playing
my scales, doing whatever it takes
to make music out of touch and air.

Sun slants through leaded glass
as it has year after year
across the seasons in this house,

but there is nothing typical about
October light or this Christmas cactus
with tight pink buds about to bloom.

Nothing typical about the whisper
of dust on the table stirred by
my footfalls as I walk to the kitchen,

imagining each mote as a planet
on which unseen creatures make their home
and wonder what life might wait

in the infinite space beyond,
their own version of dust on a table
near the window by which they kneel.

Long Distance

I knelt on the floor and started to take
jeans and shirts out of my suitcase
until I noticed I had carried the scent
of you and our house with me across
hundreds of miles and several states—
a bit of white oak and woodsmoke
from mornings you stoke the stove
before I wake, and maple-flavored
steam rising from roofs of sugar shacks
where the last sap run of the season
is being slowly boiled into syrup.
I could smell the tung-oiled, sun-warmed
barn boards used to build our table,
pots of French press we drink there
and hints of mulch and coming rain
wafting from your coat whenever you
come home from the farm at night
and kiss me hello—all of it now trapped
in the T-shirt I held to my face,
inhaling every particle of our place
and holding you close.

Light Preserves

If I had the power to preserve,
I would not trap lightning
in a bottle, would not catch even
a spark of electricity in a key
dangling from a string in a storm.

What I'd want to save for later
when winter whitens the windows
and shadows overtake the room
is the plainer blue of dawn,
brighter today for the way it presses

through the sky, behind the line
of bare, black apple trees,
their shriveled fruit encased
in skins of ice like secrets held
too long. I know this blue

will never warm me with fire.
Still, I'd store it in jars on a shelf
for the nights I wake sweating,
twisted in sheets, starved
for tomorrow's reliable light.

Darkest Before Dawn

Three days into the new year,
and despite the lack of adequate light,
our white phalaenopsis orchid
has eased open a third delicate bloom.
Perhaps coaxed by the warmth
of the woodstove a few feet away,
the orchid thrives in its tiny pot
shaped like the shell of a nautilus,
sending out new stems and glossy leaves,
its aerial roots—green at the tips—
reaching upward like tentacles
to sip the morning air. These blooms
stir something too long asleep in me,
proving with stillness and slow growth
what I haven't wanted to believe
these past few months—that hope
and grace still reign in certain sectors
of the living world, that there are laws
which can never be overturned
by hateful words or the wishes
of power-hungry men. Be patient,
this orchid seems to say, and reveal
your deepest self even in the middle
of winter, even in the darkness
before the coming dawn.

Kalokalo Volasiga

In Fijian, there is a phrase
for the last stars that appear
just before dawn, like glimpses
of past lives or those paths
never taken, making themselves
known again at the darkest hour.
I like to dream while the world
still sleeps, and tonight I wish
I had a name in my own language
for this flock of regrets, these
glittering selves I never became.
Call them the pack of sparklers
I once found hidden in a closet
months after the Fourth of July—
and see how they still glow, how
I can hold the stars in my hand
and trace my name on the air
several times before they each
burn out.

Time Capsule of the Early 21st Century

All the love songs were about
finding different ways to talk
of the sky, especially at night—
that blue before the black—
which is to say, we wanted
to pray but were too afraid
to ask for help, too busy to kneel.
We had learned to subsist
on so little hope that any scrap
was welcome, like ants clamoring
for a grain of sugar in a bowl
of nothing but salt. If you
could still see the constellations
through the ever-brightening
skyglow of light pollution,
you'd notice they were beautiful—
the glittering plan and pattern
of things not made by humans,
bodies not meant to harm.
The stars gave even the hardest
among us a hint of pleasure
as we caught a glimpse of them
through a lover's window
or while leaving a nightclub,
when we remembered to look up
long enough to be amazed.

Bluebird

I watched a bluebird flit
in and out of bittersweet vines,
knocking loose a few
of the tiny orange berries
he would later feast on.

He flies like happiness itself,
I thought at first—here
then gone then here again—
but no. That bluebird moved
like the effort it takes

to stay happy, its motion between
branches leaving a flash
of color we must hold onto
when clouds close in—
a bit of blue to weave into

each moment after snowflakes
have begun to fall like
cinders from some far-off fire
no one can contain.

Gaps

To fill the hour and leave no crevice . . . that is happiness.
—Ralph Waldo Emerson

I'd rather live in the gaps
between busy moments—

a morning without appointments
or chores like a raft

that carries me into the waters
of a calmer afternoon.

Think of the dandelions
pushing up through a crack

in the concrete, needing
just that much light

and earth to thrive—
but needing the space

to break into blossom.
Or the window I left open

an inch or so all day
so I could listen

to winter rain erasing
months of piled-up snow,

letting the grass beneath
breathe freely for a few hours

before the storm tonight
lays its heavy white sheet

over the ground again.

The Open Field

The kingdom of the instant,
the paradise of here and now:

when you choose to see
heaven as simply where you are,

it's as if a field opens up—
endless green at last revealed

beneath the gray lid of winter
lifted off the steaming earth.

The grass seems to say, *Look
what we made*, as you kneel

to take in the loamy scent
of a season rising from its bed

to switch on the lights and stoke
the fire that almost went out.

Spring Ritual

When he rises from bed with a sigh
and rubs his aching shoulders and thighs,
I know the sheets will smell of tiger balm
for weeks. But as I pry open that small jar
with the gold lid, the sudden camphor scent
makes me squint in the dim lamplight
until I see a line of farmers stretching out
behind him and around us, filling the room.

Generations pulling on patched overalls
and poorly mended jeans, thin coats reeking
of old tobacco and sweat—the same ones
they wear each spring. Then it dawns on me:
until the end of summer, most of his attention
will go into rows of freshly tilled soil
and beds of greenhouses where the purple
trumpets of eggplant flowers already peek out
from behind the vines. This is as it should be,
and as it has been for hundreds of years.

Even as I work the balm into his back,
I can see his hands itching to start the tractor
and run a rock-picker through these fields.
I can see him kneeling in the earth at the end
of a ten-hour workday and rubbing between
his fingers the fragrant leaves of a basil plant
that would not be living without him.

Ordinary Hero

The farm is the humming hive of our town
to which everyone flies in summer
when the hand-painted strawberry sign
finally appears near the pond, with red arrows
pointing the way to pick-your-own fields
of impossibly sweet, sticky-handed abundance
waiting to be plucked from vines.
You might see the owner out on a Sunday
motoring along rows of potatoes, spraying
not pesticides, but streams of powdered clay
to keep the leaf-hoppers and beetles at bay.
He'll wave to you, too, when he pulls
his hulk of a tractor off the highway
to let the line of impatient traffic pass him by.
If you're ever lucky enough to meet,
you'll know him by his outsized smile,
the way his eyes shine like two clear brooks
through which you can see to the center
of his soul, purified by this daily work
in rocky soil to which he's given his life.

Neighbors

Where I'm from, people still wave
to each other, and if someone doesn't,
you might say of her, *She wouldn't
wave at you to save her life*—

but you try anyway, give her a smile.
This is just one of the many ways
we take care of one another, say: I see you,
I feel you, I know you are real. I wave

to Rick who picks up litter while walking
his black labs, Olive and Basil—
hauling donut boxes, cigarette packs
and countless beer cans out of the brush

beside the road. And I say hello
to Christy, who leaves almond croissants
in our mailbox and mason jars of fresh-
pressed apple cider on our side porch.

I stop to check in on my mother-in-law—
more like a second mother—who buys us
toothpaste when it's on sale, and calls
if an unfamiliar car is parked at our house.

We are going to have to return to this
way of life, this giving without expectation,
this loving without conditions. We need
to stand eye to eye again, and keep asking—

no matter how busy—*How are you,
how's your wife, how's your knee?*, making
this talk we insist on calling small,
though kindness is what keeps us alive.

Kindness

It circulates like blood in us,
like rivers flowing into the ocean,
or it moves through a room
like air coaxed to blow cooler
by the blades of an oscillating fan.
It is the sweating glass of water
your lover brought and left for you
on the nightstand before bed.
It is the woman I watched once
on a plane, smoothing her daughter's
hair back from her forehead
over and over, running her fingers
through the curls until the girl
slipped into a deep sleep, resting
against her mother's shoulder.
It is the held door, the pause
that lets another go first, and you
feel the heat of it pulsing near
when a father waits patiently
while his son chooses a single ripe fig
from a bin at the grocery store
and holds it gingerly in his palm
as if it were made of blown glass
and might break open at any moment.

Claim

Stall the urge for as long as you can—
to turn on your phone, scan the headlines.
Listen instead to crickets still chirring
in long grass around the window wells, turning
their whole bodies into song. Hear a jet
roaring past overhead, ripping the afternoon
in two, and see the blue flax flowers
blooming on the hillside. Take the time
to cut a few, place them in a jamjar on the table,
though they will wilt by the end of the day.
Take delight even in the minutes spent
checking yourself for ticks, the deliberate way
you touch your own skin, as slow and tender
as a lover. Move the heavy stone of the self
away from the mouth of the cave that is
this moment, and sit in a lawnchair
in the unmown backyard, whether you are
tired or not, doing nothing but breathing in
the twin scents of raspberry blossoms
and manure spread on the fields, claiming
this entire world—mosquito, cobweb,
rust, and rain—as your own.

Spotted Wing Drosophila

Carried here on a hurricane
and kept alive by warmer winters,
these fruit flies just want to multiply,
find a home for their young.

When the slant of sun says spring,
they search for the softest skin
of cherries or nectarines to sting
and place their eggs inside.

We blame them for ruining crops,
for decimating the raspberries—
no more dew-slick jewels
hidden among thorns, no more

pies, tarts, or jams—the fruit
gone soft with rot as larvae
feed and grow inside, unaware
of the damage their living brings.

Yet like us, they have simply
staked their claim in nature,
taken over what must seem to them
nothing but ripe sites for breeding.

And don't we do the same
when we clear a tract of land
of towering pines and sumac,
of fox dens and mouse nests

and the mole's intricate tunnels,
just to build a house with a view
and move ourselves closer
to the mountains we say we love?

Orbweaver

Again I make the mistake
of thinking I'm in control
of this life, always surprised
by the call from the hospital,
the bill in the mail, the leak
sprung by a brand-new sink.
I'm like the spider weaving
her web in an open window
on the screened-in porch—
trusting such efforts will last,
never expecting some human
will come along with a rag
and in a single, merciless
act, clear away her home.
But as soon as I approach
she knows: she leaps from
screen to floor and slips
between the slats of the porch,
waiting for my heavy steps
to recede before beginning
to rebuild, in the same place,
the orb that is her world.

PART THREE

When I encounter in the great night silence before dawn the maker of music which only the heart can hear, I know that I am not alone.

—Brother David Steindl-Rast

Meditation Retreat

I remember my delight in the smallness
of the dorms we lived in that week—
the natural sound of shoes scuffing along
polished floors and carpet, doors opening
and closting. It was a relief not to have to
make eye contact or say hello to everyone
I passed in the hallway, and instead to sit
on a cushion or in my tiny room, eating
the peanuts and raisins I brought as a snack,
the taste of them never so sharp and clear
as it was during those days. We meditated
and walked, meditated and walked so much
that by 9 P.M. I fell into my twin-sized bed,
pulled up the sheets and did not wake once
until someone came through the dorm
ringing a bell the next morning. One day,
not even the bell could draw me from sleep
and film-like dreams unspooling in my fully
rested mind, and I came late to the hall,
everyone already seated on pillows, draped
in wool blankets, the hardwood floor
creaking as I stepped toward my cushion
and folded my body into that careful silence.

Natural Silence

It's not easy to find the silence
behind traffic noise and the rush of a jet
dragging its contrails through the sky.
But here it is again in the in-between,
when I learn to listen long enough
to the call-and-response of birdsong,
to wind pulsing in the canopies of trees,
and every wing-flutter of the phoebe
who's built her cup of a nest out of moss
and mud beneath the eaves of our house.
I know the stillness will last for just
a few beats before the roar of a Harley
takes over, and a tractor rumbles through
the rocky field outside my window.
So I sink into it while I can, as I do into water
so clean and clear, for a moment at least
I swear I can see to the bottom of everything.

Beginner's Mind

Everything feels so new today—
the forsythia dropping yellow petals
better than confetti around the porch

and the lime-green beginnings of leaves
popping out of buds like eager moths
brushing the hillsides with that gentle hue.

What if Emily Dickinson was right,
and we wake not older with years,
but newer every day, amazed by the jolt

of cold tiles beneath bare feet,
and sun on spring grass—have I ever
seen such green? Or the bone-white

river water chilled by snowmelt
pouring over slick rocks that seem
recently cast by some careful hand,

fired in the kiln of the warming earth.
I know this body will break down—
knees already creaking, streaks of gray

shining in my hair like spider silk—
but let me wake surprised each morning
by the familiar call of a phoebe,

tailfeathers twitching with purpose
as she perches on the porchlight and sings
the same song over and over.

Heart Song

The heart is quicker than the mind.
It tells us what to do,
and we do it without thinking.

Kiss him, it says, and we kiss.
Say this. Feel that. Offer your mother
a cup of chamomile tea
with honey, take her hand
when she's worried.

The heart says, I am tired,
and before you know it,
you've gone quiet, you've stopped
rushing along the crowded sidewalk.
Now you're touching
end-of-summer, swollen rosehips,
now you're dropping quarters
in an outstretched paper cup,
and smiling at a woman
you've never met.

We obey this mind in our chest
with its bundle of neurons,
its direct line to the actual brain
via ascending nerve pathways
faster than a bullet train.

The Japanese have two words for heart—
shinzu for the physical muscle
that does the grunt-work, the blood-work,
and *kokoro* for the mind of the heart.

The heart attracts whatever it wants,
whatever it needs, beaming out
an electromagnetic field
thousands of times more powerful
than that of the brain.

During mummification,
ancient Egyptians removed
all other organs, but left the heart
nestled in its place,
not wanting to disturb
what they believed was
the seat of the soul, the one
true brain that always knows best.

Kintsugi

Anyone who loves someone else
already has a broken heart.
It's the law: If you want that light
to flood your body, you must
expose the cracks through which
it pours, since they are the source
of your beauty and your strength.
Think of the Japanese who fill
the cracks in a ceramic bowl
with pure gold, not only flaunting
those so-called flaws, but also
making each one a priceless vein
through which light now moves.

Down to Earth

The heart of a farmer
is made of muscle
and clay that aches
for return to earth.
And when the sky
releases a steady rain,
massaging each row
of sprouted beans,
my husband leans out
of the car window
and opens his hand
to hold that water
for a single instant,
his heart now beating
in sync with rain
seeping through layers
to kiss the roots
of every plant alive
on this living, breathing
planet on whose back
we were granted
permission to live
for a limited time.

Milkweed

I can see my friend kneeling
in muddy jeans and muck boots
on the limp, frost-blasted grass,
relieved that the ground has not
yet frozen, that the rocky soil
still gives beneath her trowel
as she digs and makes space for
the milkweed seeds she plants.
She is out in the yard today
because she needs the guarantee
that at least a few of the seeds
will rise from sleep in spring
and bloom into full-blown
blossoms to feed the monarchs
who ride each thermal here,
who are not even close to extinct—
their painted parchment wings
still flashing in sunstruck air
when we need to see them most,
just when we start to believe
you can't possibly be that delicate
and still survive in this world.

Monarch

The butterfly does not break free triumphant.
Once it claws through the chrysalis,
it stands there shivering, new wings aching
as they slowly fill with blood. It must keep
its tiny eyes shut tight at first against
the brightness and shimmer of a world
it has never seen before—not like this.
It must listen until a deeper voice whispers:
The flowers are waiting. Leave the skin
of the old life far behind. Open your eyes
and give in to the blue air that will carry you
everywhere you need to go.

Cusp of Winter

These days, I look for anything
to take me back to the source—

yellow leaves splayed on the window
after a storm, like palms pressed
to the glass, trying to slip inside.

And crows calling from the upper reaches
of bare branches for the ink of evening
to spill across the sky.

Even this green bell pepper picked
before the first killing frost,
sliced on the cutting board, and tasting
of rain and loam that coddled the seed.

I'm like the toddler sneaking in
to whisper to his infant sister
through the bars of her crib:

Quick, tell me where we came from,
I'm already beginning to forget.

Swinging Door

We think we are these solid selves—
the one who stirs honey in his tea
then licks the spoon clean, the one
who stares through the skylight before bed
to count how many stars have appeared
like bright buds among the waving limbs
of maples clattering above. But what we
think of as *I* is just a swinging door
that moves back and forth each time
we inhale and exhale. I am not only
the one with a pen poised in his hand—
believing he's in control—or the one
who sends peanut butter cups and tulips
to his mother on her birthday, or the one
who looks out from an upstairs window
as his husband pulls a tarp back over
the woodpile after last night's storm.
I am not only the one who loves that
body moving in boots over pallets
placing rocks on top of the tarp to keep
the wood beneath it dry. Or the one
who watches and waits for the moment
the screen door creaks open,
slamming shut as he steps inside.

More

I know it's summer when we wade out
into the field and pick these crisp wonders,
tiny cucumbers bleached of their green
as if they've already seen too much
of this dazzling light, and can take no more.
We eat them sprinkled with salt and pepper,
as their name suggests, crunching through
flesh so sweet it's like that of a melon.
I've never seen them for sale in grocery stores,
but they grow here in this soil out of which
my husband could coax almost anything
with his sure touch and sharp attention.
He snaps them from stems with flowers still
shriveled at the ends, then hands them to me
like the gifts they are, and I take each one
into the bowl of my hands, a wandering monk
finally at home among rolling mountains
swaddled in trees, and stones heaved up
as round as eggs from sandy loam. So much
already alive between us, so many blessings
threading our days like the gold of sun—
yet here I stand, holding this bounty,
begging for more.

Acknowledgments

The author wishes to thank the Vermont Community Foundation for a generous Creation Grant from the Vermont Arts Endowment Fund, which made the writing of this book possible.

The author also thanks the editors of the following journals, magazines and newspapers in which these poems appeared, sometimes in slightly different form:

Birchsong Volume II: "Down to Earth" and "Spring Ritual"
Cascadia Review: "At Stratton Pond"
Christian Century: "Fireflies," "Night Dweller," and "Practice"
Coal Hill Review: "Tablet"
Common Ground Review: "Annunciation on Rue Saint-Urbain"
Gratefulness.org: "More"
The MacGuffin: "Milkweed"
Plough Quarterly: "Altars of Attention" and "Biblia Sacra"
Poet Lore: "Light Preserves"
Rewilding: Poems for the Environment: "Spotted Wing Drosophila"
Ruminate: "Time Capsule of the Early Twenty-First Century"
Sky Island Journal: "Kalokalo Volasiga"
Split Rock Review: "Natural Silence"
Stratton Magazine and *Vermont Magazine:* "Long Distance"
Third Wednesday: "The Price" and "Darkest Before Dawn"
The Vermont News Guide: "Rikpa," "Ripples," "Bluebird,"
   "The Open Field, "Ordinary Hero," and "Neighbors"
The Wayfarer: "Kindness"

"First Date, Hawk Mountain" also appeared in *Queer Nature* (Autumn House Press, 2021). "Long Distance" and "Down to Earth" were made into window displays for *PoemCity Vermont*, with gratitude to Rachel Senechal and the Kellogg-Hubbard Library in Montpelier for including them. "Bluebird" and "Ordinary Hero" were made into window displays for *PoemTown St. Johnsbury*, and I'm grateful to Anne Campbell and Catamount Arts for the inclusion. "Darkest Before Dawn" was also selected as a winner in *Third Wednesday's* Annual Poetry Contest (2018). "Biblia Sacra" appeared in the *Mizmor Anthology* (Poetica Publishing, 2019), with gratitude to editors, Michal Mahgerefteh and David King. "Down to Earth" and "Spring Ritual" appeared in *Birchsong: Poetry Centered in Vermont Volume II* (The Blue Line Press, 2018), with gratitude to editors Alice Wolf Gilborn, Carol Cone, David Mook, Marcia Angermann, Peter Bradley, and Monica Stillman. "Down to Earth" was also featured as part of the Poet's Corner feature in the newspapers, *The Rutland Herald* and *The Addison County Independent,* with thanks to Susan Jefts for her gorgeous writing about poetry.

I also have to thank the following for their ongoing support: Megan Mayhew Bergman and The Robert Frost Stone House at Bennington College, the Eastern Oregon University MFA program, Tracy Davies, Dafydd Wood, and Chris Morrow at the Northshire Bookstore, Jennie Rozycki and the John G. McCullough Free Library, Jenna Gersie at *The Hopper,* and Saoirse McClory, Kristi Nelson, Katie Rubinstein, Br. David Steindl-Rast, and everyone at A Network for Grateful Living. I'm also indebted to the many students who have attended my Mindfulness and Writing workshops over the years, including Ellen Perry Berkeley, Amy Bremel, Anna Chapman, Carol Cone, Alice Gilborn, Ray Hudson, Heather Newman, Mary Ellen Rudolph, and Peggy Verdi: you have all taught me far more than I could ever teach you. Special thanks to Dede Cummings for believing in me, and to the dedicated staff of Green Writers Press for producing beautiful and necessary books.

I also need to name the many friends, teachers, and colleagues whose support and encouragement have made me a better poet over the years: David Axelrod, Grace Bauer, Jennifer Boyden, Megan Buchanan, David Clewell (who started it all), Dede Cummings, Todd Davis, Chard deNiord, Pat Emile, Laura Foley, Patricia Fontaine, Margaret Hasse, Kim Hays, Jane Hirshfield, Christopher Howell, Anne Hunter, Mary Elder Jacobsen, Jesse Lee Kercheval, Samantha Kolber, Ted Kooser, Megan Kruse, Rachel Michaud, Judy Mitchell, Travis Mossotti, Stella Nelson, Amanda Noska, Naomi Shihab Nye, Erin Quick, David Romtvedt, Marge Saiser, Julia Shipley, Shari Stenberg, Heather Swan, Sam Temple, Ross Thurber, Jodi Varon, Ron Wallace, Michael Walsh, Connie Wanek, Michelle Wiegers, and Diana Whitney. Last but not least, I thank my Peacock and Crews families, and my husband, Brad Peacock, who has brought me more happiness than I ever thought possible.